RECONSTRUCTION ERA

A History from Beginning to End

Copyright © 2019 by Hourly History.

Table of Contents

Introduction

Reconstruction, the period from 1865 to 1877 that followed the end of the American Civil War, was a time of great hope in America. After the horrors of battle, people wanted to see the Union re-united and slavery—one of the key issues over which the war had been fought—abolished. Additionally, many people in the north sought the granting of civil rights and suffrage to former slaves.

The physical reconstruction of the south—the rebuilding of towns, cities, and railroads destroyed during the war—was relatively simple to achieve. The issues of emancipation and civil rights for African Americans were much more difficult to resolve. Many southerners feared that sudden freedom granted to large numbers of former slaves would undermine and perhaps destroy southern society and culture. Many reacted violently and found themselves in conflict not just with emancipated slaves, but also with their northern supporters and even the troops of the federal government.

It can be argued that Reconstruction was a failure—after 1877, the plight of many African Americans was no better than it had been in 1865. For some, it was actually worse. In another sense, Reconstruction was a success in that, by 1877, the southern states had been fully re-integrated in the Union and were playing a significant role in federal politics.

This is the story of a time of great change and great uncertainty: The Reconstruction Era.

Chapter One

Slavery and Emancipation during the Civil War

"I have always thought that all men should be free; but if any should be slaves, it should be first those who desire it for themselves, and secondly, those who desire it for others. When I hear anyone arguing for slavery, I feel a strong impulse to see it tried on him personally."

—Abraham Lincoln

The American Civil War, which was fought from 1861 to 1865, resulted in the complete military defeat of the southern Confederate States. Many people assume that the main cause of the war was slavery, with the economy of the southern states dependent on the use of slaves. The truth is that the root causes of the war were much deeper and more complex than an altruistic desire on the part of the Union to end the enslavement of African Americans. While the issue of slavery was important, it was not the main or central reason for the war, and dealing with emancipation and its consequences proved as difficult for President Lincoln and the Union during the war as it was to be after.

During his inaugural address, President Lincoln noted explicitly that he had "no purpose, directly or indirectly, to interfere with slavery in the states where it exists." When the Civil War began in 1861, he once again told Congress that this was not primarily a war to free slaves. Part of the problem was that several border states which lay between north and south but were part of the Union, including Maryland, Kentucky, and Missouri, still used slaves in agriculture and other industries. Although Lincoln personally abhorred slavery, his desire to protect the Union and to persuade the secessionist southern states to rejoin led him to downplay this aspect of the war. In the early stages, Lincoln presented the Civil War as primarily a fight to protect the Union, not a battle to free slaves.

In the early days of the war, Lincoln was also careful not to undertake any move towards emancipation which might alienate the border states or make it more difficult to persuade the Confederate States to rejoin the Union. Just five months after the war had begun, the Union Commander of the Western Department, Major General John C. Frémont, declared martial law in Missouri. The enthusiastic Frémont confiscated property belonging to owners from the Confederacy and announced that the slaves of these owners present in Missouri were to be freed. Lincoln intervened, canceling these emancipations and noting that "I think there is great danger that . . . the liberating slaves of traitorous owners, will alarm our Southern Union friends, and turn them against us." When Major General Frémont objected, he was removed from command.

When in May 1862 another Union commander, Major General David Hunter, announced the emancipation of freed slaves in South Carolina and Georgia, Lincoln intervened once again and canceled these emancipations too. It wasn't until June 1862 that Lincoln finally signed legislation that formally outlawed slavery in all U.S. territories though this was not immediately enforced.

However, as the war continued and increasing numbers of African Americans fled from the south to join the northern armies, it became obvious that the emancipation of slaves was an issue which could not be ignored. Then, in September 1862, the armies of the north and south met in battle near the small town of Sharpsburg close to the Antietam Creek in Maryland. The Confederate Army of Northern Virginia under the command of General Robert E. Lee had been attempting to invade and occupy Maryland, which remained part of the Union. They were confronted by the Potomac Army under the command of General George B. McClellan, and at around dawn on the morning of September 17, the two armies engaged in battle. Twelve hours later, almost 23,000 men were dead, wounded, or missing, and the world had been introduced for the first time to the full horror of war in the Industrial Age.

This was the largest battle of the war to date, and both sides reeled back afterward, stunned by the level of casualties sustained in a single day of fighting—to put this in context, four times more U.S. soldiers died at Antietam than died in the invasion of Normandy in World War II.

In the north, President Lincoln came under pressure to make some form of announcement about the emancipation of the thousands of African American slaves who had fled to the north. While many people shared Lincoln's moral objection to slavery, some took a much more pragmatic view; if these people were to be freed, they could then enlist in the army of the north providing an essential manpower boost in what it was becoming clear would become a war of attrition. Just five days after the Battle of Antietam, on September 22, Lincoln published a carefully worded proclamation which stated that slaves in those areas which were "in rebellion against the United States shall be then, thenceforward, and forever free."

Lincoln still had to be very careful. The phrasing of the proclamation meant that slaves in states which were part of the Confederacy would be deemed to be free only if their states were invaded by the north or if they escaped to the north. However, the status of slaves in states which were part of the Union such as Maryland and Kentucky was unchanged. African American slaves in the southern states saw this proclamation as a promise of freedom if they could escape from the south and enter the northern states. Over the next three years, more than half a million slaves made their way north to freedom. This not only deprived the Confederacy of essential workers, but it also provided a vital source of new troops for the Union. Almost 200,000 African Americans, many former slaves, joined the armies of the north and fought bravely during the remainder of the Civil War.

However, even Lincoln did not envisage freed African Americans becoming part of the United States after the Civil War. Instead he favored a policy of colonization, where freed slaves would be encouraged to emigrate to form their own nations, perhaps in Central or South America. Lincoln's reasons for this were clear—he did not feel that former slaves would be treated well or allowed to integrate into primarily white societies either in the north or the south. At around the same time he was drafting the

Proclamation of Emancipation, Lincoln met with African American leaders and pressed his plan for the creation of colonies. He promised that these colonies would be protected by the United States, and some African Americans were persuaded to go to Haiti and Chiriqui, a province of Panama in Central America. However, neither colony proved able to become self-sufficient, and there were no further attempts to send freed slaves outside the United States.

These events show that Lincoln was thinking about the problems associated with the assimilation of freed slaves into American society well before the war ended. There is evidence to suggest that Lincoln never completely abandoned his idea of sending freed people to some remote place beyond the borders of the United States and that his intention was to resurrect this idea once the war was ended.

Chapter Two

The End of Abraham Lincoln and the Civil War

"The restoration of the Rebel States to the Union must rest upon the principle of civil and political equality of both races; and it must be sealed by general amnesty."

—Abraham Lincoln

The Civil War was the most traumatic event of the nineteenth century for Americans. As many as three-quarters of a million soldiers may have died during the conflict, the equivalent of around two percent of the total population of America in 1861. More than 400,000 men were left severely wounded. Much of the fighting, particularly towards the end of the war, took place in the southern states and many of these were left devastated. Several southern cities, including Atlanta, Georgia and Richmond, Virginia (the capital of the Confederacy), were destroyed either as a result of fighting or as part of a deliberate policy of destruction intended to undermine the morale of the south. Infrastructure such as railroads was destroyed as were many plantations and farms.

However, the most severe damage to the south was that caused to its economic and agricultural systems. After the Civil War, Confederate money became virtually worthless almost overnight. Food shortages and rampant inflation during the latter stages of the Civil War and immediately after caused great hardship in the Confederate States. Even more fundamentally, the abolition of slavery in the south changed and undermined the capacity of those states to generate wealth and even to produce food. Many of the northern states had embraced industrialization where machines did a great deal of the work. In the south, many agricultural processes and even some industries were predicated on the availability of cheap labor in the form of slaves. When this source of labor was suddenly removed, many southern businesses were no longer viable.

The Civil War also moved the political balance of power in America towards the northern states. During 50 of the 72 years from the adoption of the United States Constitution in 1789 to the outbreak of the Civil War in 1861, America had a president from one of the southern, slave-owning states. After the Civil War, it would be 100 years before a person from one of the former Confederate States would be elected president of the United States.

As early as 1863, major Union victories at battles in Gettysburg and Vicksburg made it apparent that the north would most likely emerge victorious, and in that year President Lincoln issued a Proclamation of Amnesty and Reconstruction. Even during the war it was clear that Lincoln was thinking about the post-war situation and how the former Confederate States could be drawn back into the Union. By this time, the issue of slavery and its abolition had become an important war aim for the north, and it was obvious that the southern states would have to be helped and encouraged to develop an economy which was not based on the availability of slave labor.

The Proclamation of 1863 promised the restoration of confiscated property and full pardons for all but the highest levels of the Confederate administration. It also allowed that new state governments could be established in the southern states when at least ten percent of the eligible voters had sworn an oath of allegiance to the United States. These were generous concessions from a leader who was heading for total victory, but the proclamation also confirmed that slavery was to be abolished throughout the United States and that the former Confederate States were responsible for ensuring the welfare of former slaves.

Some Radical Republicans in the north were unhappy as they believed that the process of Reconstruction and reconciliation proposed by the president was too lenient on the rebellious southern states, but the respect felt by most people in the north for Lincoln was so great that there was little real dissent. Under the leadership of Abraham Lincoln, it seemed that once the fighting was finally over, a process of healing and reconciliation would begin in the United States.

Lincoln's approach was based on forgiveness and reconciliation, but it was also pragmatic—by making a very public statement about the post-war situation, he hoped to persuade the Confederate States to surrender. This didn't happen, and an increasingly vocal minority of Radical Republicans in Congress continued to demand that the south should be punished after the war. These people wanted to see the complete destruction of southern society and the emancipation of all former slaves.

Even before the war ended, the state of Louisiana attempted to draft a new constitution in 1864 based on the president's proclamation. Louisiana was one of the Confederate States, but it was occupied by Union troops, and the legislature there drafted a new constitution promising the abolition of slavery, free schooling, and a program of public works. Lincoln approved the new constitution but Congress, dominated by Radical Republicans intent on punishment, refused to recognize it, and members who were elected in Louisiana in 1864 were not allowed to sit in Congress.

In the summer of 1864, the same Radical Republicans who had vetoed the Louisiana constitution attempted to push a new piece of legislation through Congress—the Wade-Davis Bill. This was a direct challenge to Lincoln's Proclamation and insisted that former Confederate States could only rejoin the Union if at least 50 percent of eligible voters were willing to swear an "ironclad oath" of allegiance to the United States. The new bill also introduced safeguards for black civil liberties, though it stopped short of giving African Americans the vote.

Concerned that the passing of such a bill might persuade the Confederate States to prolong the war, President Lincoln was able to use Congressional convention to veto the Wade-Davis Bill, but he was not able to silence the growing power of the Radical Republicans. The disagreement between the president and Congress extended to the redistribution of land to former slaves after the war. While Lincoln was willing to see some land which had been taken from southern estates given to former slaves, the Radicals in Congress sought something more fundamental. Against the president's objections, Congress established the Freedmen's Bureau in early 1865. The purpose of this new organization was to distribute food and supplies in former Confederate territories occupied by the Union, to build and staff schools, and redistribute land confiscated from southern estates to former slaves and poor whites.

While Congress regarded this as a perfectly reasonable step towards the reconstruction of the southern states in a form more acceptable to the rest of the Union, the Freedmen's Bureau was viewed by many southerners as a threat to their way of life, especially when it became known that the Bureau was willing to assign 40 acres of confiscated land to anyone willing to swear an oath of allegiance to the United States and the tenant would have the option to purchase this land at a later date.

In February 1865, there was a peace conference between senior leaders of the Confederacy and the leaders of the Union. The southern leaders suggested, amongst other things, that they would be willing to accept a position of servitude for African Americans rather than outright slavery. Lincoln rejected this suggestion completely, telling the delegates from the Confederacy unequivocally that "Slavery is doomed!" It was clear that the post-war period was likely to see intense conflict between Lincoln and his desire for reconciliation, the Radical Republicans who wanted to see punishment and the complete replacement of the institutions and systems of the southern states, and the leaders of the southern states who wanted as little change as possible.

By April of 1865, the war was drawing to a close. On April 9, the most successful and influential Confederate general, Robert E. Lee, surrendered in the village of Appomattox Court House in Virginia. As they heard about the surrender of the largest Confederate army, other Confederate units also began to surrender. The Civil War was almost over, and most people expected that a showdown between President Lincoln and the Hawks in Congress was about to begin.

Then, on the evening of April 14, 1865, President Lincoln decided to go to Ford's Theatre in Washington, D.C. to watch a new play, *Our American Cousin*, with his wife Mary and some friends. The Lincolns arrived late, and when they took their seats, the play was interrupted as the orchestra played *Hail to the Chief* and the whole audience rose to applaud the president. Lincoln had never been more popular or more respected, and most people believed that his policy of reconciliation with the former Confederate States would prevail over the punishment advocated by his opponents.

At around 10:25, while Lincoln was laughing at the play, well-known actor John Wilkes Booth entered the president's box and shot him in the head with a small pistol. Abraham Lincoln died in the early hours of the following morning, and the face of American politics was completely and irreversibly changed.

Chapter Three

President Johnson and the first Black Codes

"I must be permitted to say that I have been almost overwhelmed by the announcement of the sad event which has so recently occurred. I feel incompetent to perform duties so important and responsible as those which have been so unexpectedly thrown upon me."

—Andrew Johnson

With the assassination of Abraham Lincoln, Vice President Andrew Johnson suddenly became president of the United States, inheriting all the problems of reconciliation that the previous president had faced but without the legacy of respect and approval that Lincoln had enjoyed.

Part of the problem was that many people regarded Johnson as a drunkard. On March 4, 1865, Johnson had given his first speech to the Senate. It didn't go well. The speech was rambling and, at times, completely incoherent, and it was clear to everybody watching that Johnson was more than a little drunk. Unconcerned, Lincoln made a statement a few days later in which he noted that "I have known Andy Johnson for many years; he made a bad slip the other day, but you need not be scared; Andy ain't a drunkard." Despite this reassurance, many people were concerned at Johnson's fitness to assume the role of president.

Johnson was sworn in on the morning of April 15, 1865, and to the relief of everybody present, his demeanor was said by newspaper reporters who were present to have been "solemn and dignified." Johnson continued with many of the policies pursued by his predecessor. In the final days of Lincoln's presidency, Congress had approved what would become the Thirteenth Amendment to the United States Constitution. However, this would not become law until it had been ratified by the requisite number of states. Johnson pushed through this legislation, and the Thirteenth Amendment became part of the U.S. Constitution on December 6, 1965. This amendment abolished slavery in every state, including the defeated southern states but also in the border states which had supported the Union during the war.

However, merely abolishing slavery did not mean that African Americans suddenly became equal citizens of the United States. Johnson's view was that it was not up to the federal government to impose their view on how freed slaves should be treated and that this should instead be left to individual state legislatures to decide. Johnson appointed new governors in many southern states, and the only things that he demanded of these new governors were that they repudiate demands for secession and ensure that the Thirteenth Amendment was enacted within their states. In most southern states, this was done—but in such a way as to ensure that freedmen continued to be treated as second-class citizens and denied many of the rights that whites enjoyed.

Several southern states created Black Codes, pieces of legislation intended to ensure that African Americans remained at the bottom of the social order and continued to provide low-cost labor on southern plantations. Black Codes restricted the rights of African Americans to own property, to conduct business, to bear arms, and even to move freely in public places. However, a central element of these codes was the notion of vagrancy as a social issue. The idea of large numbers of unemployed former slaves with time on their hands was seen by many southerners to be a threat to the very fabric of society. Any African American who did not have a job (or at least, was not working in a position recognized by white people as permanent employment) was committing a criminal offense and was liable to arrest and imprisonment. Failure to pay taxes or breaking any one of a whole series of minor laws could also see an African American classed as a vagrant and imprisoned. In order to avoid an accusation of vagrancy, African Americans had to be employed under an annual labor contract and had to be able to produce a copy of this on demand.

These draconian new laws were combined with changes in the legislation relating to the system state penitentiaries. These introduced convict leasing, a system where state prisons were permitted to hire out convicts as laborers on state and private works. In practice, this gave state law enforcement agencies a strong incentive to arrest African Americans on vagrancy laws. Once incarcerated, these people could then be provided as unpaid labor to plantation owners and others. The person or organization taking on such prisoners was responsible for providing secure accommodation as well as food for these unpaid workers. This provided employers with employees who cost as little as slaves, and many of these workers were kept in appalling conditions. For the state, this removed the need to build prisons or to feed prisoners. The system was so successful that some southern states did not need to build prisons until the 1890s.

In states where the Black Codes were brought in, the plight of African Americans changed little from the time when they were slaves. In some ways, it became even worse—slaves were valuable property and could be re-sold when times were hard, so it made sense to keep them in good health. If a prisoner became ill or even died as a result of mistreatment, the state would simply provide another. Historian Samuel McCall wrote in 1899 that Black Codes had "established a condition but little better than that of slavery, and in one important respect far worse: by severing the property relationship, they had diminished the incentive for property owners to ensure the relative health and survival of their workers."

The first Black Code was enacted in Mississippi in an ironically titled piece of legislation: *An Act to confer Civil Rights on Freedmen.* This act required all African American men to present an annual labor contact in January each year. Failure to do so would result in classification as a vagrant and arrest. Workers who reneged on their annual contracts were treated as runaways who could be classed as vagrants. Even whites who associated with or assisted African Americans could find themselves arrested for vagrancy. The Mississippi code was quickly amended to include a clause which noted that "all white persons so assembling themselves with freedmen, free negroes or mulattoes, or usually associating with freedmen, free negroes or mulattoes, on terms of equality, shall be deemed vagrants."

The Black Code enacted in Mississippi became the model for others that followed, and South Carolina, Alabama, and Louisiana all introduced their own Black Codes in late 1865. In early 1866, Florida, Virginia, Georgia, North Carolina, Texas, Tennessee, and Arkansas all followed the leads of these states. Thomas W. Conway, the commissioner for the Freedmen's Bureau in Louisiana noted in 1866, "These codes were simply the old black code of the state, with the word 'slave' expunged, and 'Negro' substituted. The most odious features of slavery were preserved in them."

The creation of the Black Codes led to outrage in the north. It seemed to many people that the southern states were attempting to ignore one of the fundamental objectives of the Civil War—the abolition of slavery. During 1866, Congress passed several pieces of significant legislation aimed at producing real change in the southern states.

The Civil Rights Act of 1866 had first been passed by Congress in 1865, but President Johnson, fearing further alienation of the southern states, had vetoed it. In April 1866, the bill was once again passed by Congress and once again vetoed by the president. However, a two-thirds majority in each chamber supported the act, and it became law without the approval or signature of the president. The purpose of the act was to define what was meant by citizenship in the United States and to affirm that all laws applied equally to all citizens, effectively making the Black Codes illegal.

Concurrent with the passage of the Civil Rights Act, Congress also approved the Fourteenth Amendment to the United States Constitution. This amendment also sought to define citizenship and to ensure that all laws and statues applied equally to all citizens. This amendment was bitterly contested in Congress by the southern states who recognized that it was incompatible with the Black Codes. The amendment was quickly ratified by most of the northern states, but it did not finally become a part of the U.S. Constitution until the middle of 1868—some southern states were only persuaded to ratify this amendment when this was made a condition of their joining Congress. President Johnson was utterly opposed to this amendment and not only tried unsuccessfully to block it in Congress, he openly encouraged the southern states not to ratify it.

Also in 1866, Congress passed a second Freedman's Bureau Bill which gave additional rights to former slaves including the right to own property, access to schools, and the right to appeal to a military court if these rights were not upheld by state legislature. This bill was opposed by President Johnson and supported by Republicans in Congress. The president attempted to veto this bill, but it gained the required majority on both chambers and was passed without the president's signature.

The Civil War might have been over and, officially at least, slavery might have been abolished across the United States, but it was clear that the questions of the status and rights of former slaves were far from agreed across the country. Bitter disputes followed and before long these arguments erupted into savage violence.

Chapter Four

Radical Reconstruction

"The attempt to place the white population under the domination of persons of color in the South has impaired, if not destroyed, the kindly relations that had previously existed between them: and mutual distrust has engendered a feeling of animosity which leading in some instances to collision and bloodshed, has prevented that cooperation between the two races so essential to the success of industrial enterprise in the Southern States."

—Andrew Johnson

The events of 1865 had made it clear that there were fundamental differences between the approach to Reconstruction of President Johnson and that of the Radicals in Congress, who felt that the president was in danger of negating all the sacrifices made during the Civil War by allowing southern states to continue to discriminate against African American in the most blatant way. The president felt that it was more important to encourage the former Confederate States back into the Union and to avoid any course of action that would make this more difficult. Then, in early May 1866, racial tensions erupted into violence in the state of Tennessee.

In the city of Memphis, the population of African Americans was substantial, perhaps as many as 20,000 by

1865, out of a total population of around 35,000. Many were former slaves, and a proportion were former soldiers of the Union Army. The white authorities in Memphis used vagrancy laws to arrest many African Americans and applied convict leasing to force many of these people to work on plantations. This caused anger and resentment in African American communities in the city, and on May 1, 1866, a large group of African Americans including ex-soldiers, women, and children gathered in a public space to hold a street party. Alarmed by this large gathering, the city recorder ordered police officers to break up the gathering.

People refused to disperse, and the small party of police officers was confronted by much larger numbers of ex-soldiers. One of the police officers accidentally shot himself in the leg. A firefight then began between the remaining police officers, assisted by a group of armed whites, and the African Americans. One police officer was shot dead during this exchange of fire. That evening, a mob of armed whites attacked African American areas of the city, burning buildings and killing many blacks. Over the course of the next couple of days, 46 African Americans were killed, 75 were injured, and 4 churches and 12 schools used by African Americans were destroyed by fire as were many homes. No criminal charges were ever raised against any person who had taken part in the rioting.

These events, which became known as the Memphis Massacre, caused anger and consternation in the north. They also helped to further undermine the position of President Johnson who was himself from Tennessee. Three months later, another riot, this time in New Orleans, left 44

African Americans dead and many more wounded and led to the imposition of martial law in the city.

The imposition of Black Codes and the massacres in Memphis and New Orleans led many people to look toward a much more radical form of Reconstruction than the one suggested and supported by President Johnson. In elections for the House of Representative and Senate in 1866, Radical Republicans won over 75 percent of seats in Congress. This period became known as Radical Reconstruction and led directly in 1867 to the passing of the Reconstruction Acts, four pieces of legislation intended to force the southern states to change their treatment of former slaves.

In July 1867, the Reconstruction Acts were used as the basis for creating military control over ten former Confederate States (all but Tennessee which had agreed to ratify the Fourteenth Amendment). Over 20,000 US troops were sent to the south, and state governments were reconstituted under the direct control of military commanders. Effectively, the ten southern states were placed under martial law.

The Radicals in Congress who had pushed for military rule in the south wanted it there, in part, to ensure that freed slaves who had been given the vote were able to vote freely in elections. Only in this way, they believed, could African Americans finally achieve equality with whites. However, though the military councils were supposed to be ensuring fairness, many southerners felt that they were actually doing the precise opposite. The Reconstruction Acts called for the registration of all adult males who were eligible to vote. But there were exceptions—the most notable being that the vote was to be extended to all males "except those who had ever sworn an oath to uphold the Constitution of the United States and then engaged in rebellion." In some southern states, military councils took this to mean that all men who had formerly been officers in the Confederate Army, state or city officeholders, or even employees of a Confederate state or city administration were not eligible to vote.

Taking into account these exceptions, many white men were barred from voting, and this skewed electoral rolls in some states. In Texas, for example, African American men accounted for around 30% of the male population. However, the disenfranchisement of large numbers of white men who had been involved in city or state administration meant that African Americans accounted for over 45% of eligible voters in Texas. These measures provoked anger amongst whites in the southern states and unease amongst many in the north. Disenfranchisement for those who had previously served the Confederacy clearly did not equate to equality and the universal male suffrage that many felt were intrinsic to the Constitution of the United States.

Tensions increased in the southern states as positions became entrenched and soon, new derogatory words would enter the political lexicon in the United States: carpetbagger and scalawag.

Chapter Five

Carpetbaggers and Scalawags

"A few white scalawags were seen to approach the polls during the day, most of them throwing furtive glances to the right and left to see if their presence in the ebony crowd was noticed."

—Report on an election in 1867 in Augusta, Georgia in the *Chronicle & Sentinel* newspaper

The word "carpetbagger" had been in use in the United States for some time by the end of the Civil War. It was used to denote a traveler who arrived in a new area with his possessions in a satchel made from pieces of carpet. After the war, it took on a new and more derogatory meaning. The term was used to describe people from the north who came to the southern states in the period immediately after the war in the hope of establishing businesses. Many were businessmen who hoped to buy or lease land or plantations or to find southern partners with whom they could work to rebuild the process of producing cotton.

Initially, such people were welcomed in the south, as they brought much-needed cash which helped to re-establish the economy. Yet before long, this perception changed and northern incomers became viewed as parasites who hoped to become rich by taking advantage of the misfortune of the south. The truth was more complex. Some northerners who came south after the Civil War were rapacious businessmen who believed they could turn a short-term profit from the chaos left by the war. Others were genuine reformers who believed that it would be possible to change southern society to make it more similar to the north—amongst many northerners, there was a belief that the north was more advanced than the south and that people from the north had a moral obligation to help improve the south.

Many of these altruistic northerners found work with the new Freedmen's Bureaus or took jobs as teachers and journalists in the hope of changing entrenched attitudes. In time, the term carpetbagger came to be applied to any northerner who arrived in the south in the years after the Civil War, and most came to be regarded with suspicion and distrust by the people of the south. Still, there was one thing even more despised in the south than a carpetbagger, and that was a scalawag.

The word "scalawag" was originally used in the United States to denote a farm animal of no use or value. It later came to mean an untrustworthy person of no worth. After the end of the Civil War, it took on a new and very specific meaning in the southern states. Not everyone in the south had supported the Confederacy during the Civil War. Conservatives in the south had believed that African Americans should not be slaves and should be entitled to vote, though most seem to have believed that there should still be a white-dominated political system. After the Civil War, these people were joined by non-slave owning small farmers as well as businessmen and professional people who had remained loyal to the Union throughout the war. Some of these people had left the south during the war to serve with the Union; some had been imprisoned in the south for their Unionist views. Not all were idealists—many of these people were fervently anti-black, but they had all opposed the rebellion, and all were generally minded to go along with the reconstruction plans of the Radical Republicans.

Southerners who supported Reconstruction generally became known as scalawags and represented as many as 20% of eligible white voters in the upper south, and they quickly became a significant force in southern politics. For many southerners, these were traitors who were despised even more than carpetbaggers.

In 1867 and 1868, the ten southern states under military control held constitutional conventions to establish how these states would be administered under universal male suffrage. For the first time, these conventions included African American voters. Many scalawags and some carpetbaggers wanted to use these conventions to exclude former Confederate supporters and to take the opportunity to fundamentally change southern society. However, perhaps more inclined to recall the unfairness of the previous system, many African Americans were opposed to any form of exclusion and favored allowing all men, white and black, to have the vote. Carpetbaggers used the conventions to attract financial aid from the north, particularly to fund the reconstruction of the railroad system in the south which had been largely destroyed during the war. Many of the conventions also established free public schools, though these were not required to be integrated.

Unfortunately, the conventions did not produce conclusive results and failed to completely satisfy anyone. Many southerners felt that they were being forced to accept disproportionate numbers of black voters, often by the hated scalawags and carpetbaggers. Many Radical Republicans felt that Reconstruction was not proceeding quickly enough or integrating African Americans into the social and political structure of the south as they wanted.

The Fifteenth Amendment to the United States Constitution was proposed in February 1869, and this legislated that no person could be refused the right to vote on the basis of "race, color, or previous condition of servitude." This wasn't quite the same as guaranteeing ex-slaves the vote—the drawing up of electoral rolls and setting laws governing elections were still the responsibility of individual states, but it was intended to ensure that it would not be possible to discriminate against any potential voter purely on the basis of race.

By the time that this amendment came into force, the divisions between the Radical Republicans and President Johnson had become so apparent and so intractable that the Republicans had decided to adopt a new, more suitable candidate for the next presidential election.

Chapter Six

Ulysses S. Grant Takes the Presidency

"Everyone has his superstitions. One of mine has always been when I started to go anywhere, or to do anything, never to turn back or to stop until the thing intended was accomplished."

—Ulysses S. Grant

Divisions between President Johnson and the Republican majority in Congress came to a head in March 1868 when the House of Representatives attempted to impeach the president. The formal issue was a dispute over supposed breaches of the Tenure of Office Act; the real reason was a growing feeling amongst Republicans that Reconstruction could not proceed as they wanted while Johnson was president.

This was the first time that a U.S. president had been impeached, and at a Senate trial at the end of March attended by 54 members from 27 states, the vote was 35 votes for guilty and 19 for not guilty. The Constitution required a two-thirds majority if the president was to be impeached, and this result fell just one vote short of that threshold. Johnson remained in office, but his relationship with the House of Representatives was irrevocably damaged. It wasn't long before Republicans began looking for another nominee for president who could win the election of 1868.

General Ulysses S. Grant had been one of the most effective and successful northern military leaders during the Civil War, and he was seen as personally responsible for the defeat of the most outstanding Confederate general, Robert E. Lee. After the war, Grant served as Commanding Officer of the U.S. Army and for a short time as Secretary of War under President Johnson. However, Grant and Johnson disagreed over several issues, including Reconstruction—Grant was in favor of more radical Reconstruction than the cautious Johnson.

In May of 1868, at the Republican National Convention, Grant was nominated unopposed to be the Republican presidential candidate in the forthcoming election. Grant was opposed in the election by the Democratic nominee, Horatio Seymour. Grant won easily—he won the Electoral College victory by 214 votes to 80 and gained over 52 percent of the popular vote. In March 1869, Grant was sworn-in as the 18th president of the United States. He was also the youngest at age 46, and in his inaugural address he promised that he would continue the process of Reconstruction "calmly, without prejudice, hate or sectional pride."

Soon after his inauguration, Grant pressed Congress to formally readmit the states of Virginia, Mississippi, and Texas into the Union. All three had established new state constitutions which guaranteed all eligible males the vote, regardless of color or former servitude. Grant also signed into law a bill from Congress for the establishment of what would become the United States Department of Justice, a federal department responsible for the enforcement of the law and the administration of justice throughout the United States.

Grant also pushed for the state ratification of the Fifteenth Amendment, and in February 1870, the amendment achieved the required number of ratifications by states and became part of the U.S. Constitution. Grant called this "a measure of grander importance than any other one act of the kind from the foundation of our free government to the present day." Early in his presidency, Grant met with and consulted leaders of African American communities and pushed through a bill which guaranteed equal rights to blacks in Washington, D.C.

Three new bills, the Enforcement Acts, were passed through Congress in 1870-1871. These were codes which made it a criminal offense to deny any former slave the right to vote, to serve on juries, or to hold state or federal office. Crucially, these acts included the right of the federal government to intervene if states proved unwilling or unable to enforce these new laws.

These Enforcement Acts were important because it was becoming clear that some people were prepared to use violence to block African Americans from voting.

Chapter Seven

The Rise of the Ku Klux Klan

"Bands of men, masked and armed, made their appearance; White Leagues and other societies were formed; large quantities of arms and ammunition were imported and distributed to these organizations; military drills, with menacing demonstrations, were held, and with all these murders enough were committed to spread terror among those whose political action was to be suppressed, if possible, by these intolerant and criminal proceedings."

—Ulysses S. Grant

Across the south, many former slaves formed new churches. They left the predominantly white churches which already existed and created their own, new, mainly Baptist or Methodist churches. By 1871, Northern Baptist churches alone had more than 80,000 black members in the south, and ministers of these churches became important and respected community leaders.

However, in many southern states, whites were beginning to band together in semi-secret organizations intended to limit the growth of black political and social power. One of the most prominent of these was the Ku Klux Klan (KKK), initially founded in 1865 as a form of social club for former members of the Confederate armies—its first leader was Nathan Bedford Forrest, a former general of the Confederate Army. Before long, the KKK became directly involved in the politics of Reconstruction in the south.

On the pretext that they were maintaining law and order, members of this organization began to target African Americans using violence and intimidation. Many blacks were brutally beaten for offenses including "impudence" to white people. Teachers at schools for children of former slaves were whipped if it was felt that their teaching promoted Republicanism, and many schoolhouses were burned.

During the elections of 1868, the activities of the KKK reached new levels. Black voters were not just intimidated; they were murdered on a large scale. In Louisiana, more than 1,000 African Americans were murdered during the election campaign. In Kansas, there were more than 2,000 murders. In Georgia, there were more than 300 murders or assaults intended to kill, and whippings and beatings became almost commonplace not just of African Americans but also of scalawags and carpetbaggers who were seen as supporting the rise of black political power. In all three of these states, Republicans were soundly beaten in the elections as a direct result of this intimidation.

The KKK wasn't the only white supremacist organization operating in the south at this time—the Knights of the White Camellia, for example, was founded in Louisiana in 1867 with similar aims, but the KKK was the most widespread and had the largest membership. It was said that at this time in Alabama, around one in every nine white voters was a member of the Klan.

When the Enforcement Acts were passed into law (making any interference with elections a criminal offense), these were primarily targeted at the KKK. Although the KKK wasn't able to prevent the election of Ulysses S. Grant, by 1870, the organization had members in almost every southern state and its hooded and masked members attacked and intimidated seemingly at will. Klan membership ranged from the poorest whites to lawyers and even ministers of white churches. Membership in law enforcement organizations and the judiciary was also widespread in the south, making it very difficult to arrest and convict members of the KKK.

In July 1870, members of the KKK killed six African Americans, including a teacher, at Cross Plains in Calhoun County, Alabama. During a grand jury hearing into these killings, other African Americans who had been present identified the murderers by name. The all-white grand jury declined to proceed with any prosecutions. In January 1871, over five hundred masked members of the KKK attacked the Union County Jail in South Carolina, and eight black prisoners were dragged outside and brutally lynched. No-one was ever arrested or charged with any offense following this attack.

Part of the problem was the secrecy and mystery with which the KKK invested itself. No-one was ever quite sure who was or wasn't a member, and the perception of the reach and extent of the organization was probably much greater than the reality. The other issue was that many people in the southern states covertly supported the brutal violence of the Klan, even if they were not members and took no part themselves. The Klan was seen both as a method of preventing lawlessness amongst former slaves (a prospect that terrified the white population of some states) and as a form of guerrilla movement fighting against the military rule imposed by the north.

Increasing violence led directly to the passing of the Third Enforcement Act of 1871, widely known as the Ku Klux Klan Act. This act empowered the president to use federal troops to enforce the law and to have people suspected of racially motivated crimes to be tried in federal courts (where juries were often predominantly black). President Grant used this unprecedented expansion of federal power to employ the U.S. Army to support federal marshals in attacking the KKK in South Carolina and elsewhere.

President Grant's campaign against the KKK proved very effective. Many hundreds of its members were brought to trial and sent to prison. Membership declined rapidly in the early 1870s though some former Klansmen went on to join other secret white supremacist organizations such as the White League. Despite all its efforts, the KKK was unable to stop Reconstruction. Yet by the time that the Klan was being virtually destroyed, there were other even more powerful factors which were conspiring to limit efforts of ensuring the equality of African Americans in the southern states.

Chapter Eight

Corruption and Recession

"Looking back over the whole policy of reconstruction, it seems to me that the wisest thing would have been to have continued for some time the military rule. Sensible Southern men see now that there was no government so frugal, so just, and fair as what they had under our generals."

—Ulysses S. Grant

Although President Grant appears to have been entirely honest, his administration was weakened and tainted by scandal and corruption almost from the start. The first, the Black Friday Gold Panic, happened in 1869, just months after Grant came to office. A pair of ruthless Wall Street speculators, Jay Gould and James Fisk, invented a scheme to make money through buying and selling gold. To make the scheme work, it was necessary to persuade the president to temporarily stop selling U.S. Treasury gold.

The president was persuaded that this would be good for the economy, the scheme went ahead, and the two speculators made a great deal of money. The ensuing gold panic weakened the U.S. economy for many months. During a Congressional investigation later in 1869, it was found that the two speculators had paid the Assistant Secretary to the Treasury a bribe of $10,000. It was also claimed that the First Lady, Julia Grant, had received a package containing $25,000, though this was not proved. This scandal and several others which followed tainted the administration of Grant—although none of the scandals directly related to the president himself, it did seem that he was more than a little naïve in selecting and controlling the members of his administration.

Growing dissatisfaction with Grant over allegations of corruption and the increasing use of federal troops in the south was a contributory factor to a split which began to develop in the Republican Party. In the elections of 1872, a new political party appeared, the Liberal Republicans, a group who were committed to the continuation of Radical Reconstruction and the ending of political violence in the south. Membership of the new party came mainly from dissatisfied Radical Republicans and included the editors and owners of several large newspapers. One of these editors, Horace Greeley, founder and editor of the *New York Tribune*, became the new party's nomination for the presidential elections, standing against Grant. Even though Greeley also attracted support from Democrats, Grant won the election and was re-elected to serve for another four years.

After the election, the Liberal Republican Party dissolved, and many Republicans who had previously been ardent supporters of Radical Reconstruction abandoned their support. Even in the south, Republican groups which had previously been united began to split. Radical Republicans and Liberal Republicans began squabbling in several states, and this in-fighting allowed Democrats to take power in several places. African American voters were also unhappy because they did not feel that Republican politicians had delivered on their promises, particularly assurances about the re-distribution of land.

On the other side, the Democrats were also changing. Some disaffected Republicans, angered by the failure of Reconstruction and continuing political violence, formed new Conservative parties, many of which became affiliated with the Democratic Party. Political violence continued across the south. In the Colfax Massacre of 1873, up to 150 African American men were murdered by whites following a contested election. In 1874, over 5,000 armed members of the White League battled successfully with police and militia before occupying federal offices in New Orleans for three days.

Many people within the Democratic Party were coming to believe that this violence achieved little beyond causing misery and suffering and that it was time for the party to accept Reconstruction and to fight the Republicans on issues other than race and black emancipation. From 1870, many Democrats embraced the New Departure, a policy in which the Democrats claimed to be just as loyal to the Union as Republicans, but more able to run the economy efficiently. The party also quietly dropped opposition to some African American rights. Democrats who supported the New Departure became known as Redeemers, and they were very successful in eroding support in the south and the north for Republicans who they attacked as complacent, corrupt, and inefficient.

The Democratic Party's claims of financial mismanagement seemed to be justified in 1873 when the U.S. economy entered a severe recession following a world-wide financial crisis, the Panic of 1873. President Grant was blamed for not avoiding the effects of the recession in America. In the elections of 1874, the Republican Party lost heavily, and conservative Democrats (now known as Bourbon Democrats) took control of the House. By 1874, only three southern states, Louisiana, Mississippi and South Carolina, were still controlled by Republican administrations—all the others had fallen to the Democrats.

Chapter Nine

The End of Reconstruction

"Let me assure my countrymen of the Southern States that it is my earnest desire to regard and promote their truest interest—the interests of the white and of the colored people both and equally—and to put forth my best efforts in behalf of a civil policy which will forever wipe out in our political affairs the color line and the distinction between North and South, to the end that we may have not merely a united North or a united South, but a united country."

—Rutherford B. Hayes

Violence continued to be an intrinsic part of politics in the southern states. Although the KKK had been suppressed, new white supremacist movements had arisen such as the White League and the Red Shirts in Mississippi and South Carolina. Attacks on Republican politicians and former slaves continued as did violence against any person considered to be supporting Reconstruction or African American rights—in Louisiana, a judge and district attorney were murdered in 1873. In August 1874, an armed group of members of the White League seized a number of white republicans and black former slaves in Coushatta in Red River Parish, Louisiana. Six of the whites and twenty freedmen were subsequently murdered. No-one was ever brought to trial for any of these murders.

In 1875, state elections in Mississippi brought even worse violence. In the city of Vicksburg, there were large numbers of black voters, and the city had even elected an African American sheriff. Members of the Red Shirts supported by other white supremacist groups descended on to the city to try to suppress black voting in the August election. Parties of armed whites patrolled the streets during the election to prevent African Americans from casting votes. As a direct result, Democratic candidates were elected in almost every position.

By December, the situation in the city had become so hazardous for blacks that the sheriff was forced to flee. Groups of armed whites arrived in the city, and over the course of the next few days, as many as 300 blacks were murdered in the city and surrounding areas. When the governor of Mississippi, Adelbert Ames, asked the president to send federal troops to end the violence, Grant initially refused, claiming that people were "tired out" by continual political violence in the south. Finally, the president relented, and federal troops were used to escort the sheriff back into Vicksburg where he too was murdered a few days later.

Violence in the south continued during the 1876 presidential election. The Republican nominee in the election was Rutherford B. Hayes, a relatively unknown politician from Ohio. Hayes stood against the Democratic nominee, Samuel J. Tilden, in what was to become one of the most challenged and closely contested presidential elections ever. Three days after the election, Tilden held 184 electoral votes, just one short of a majority. Hayes had only 166 votes, but there were 19 still to be confirmed from the states of Florida, Louisiana, and South Carolina. Hayes needed all 19 if he was to become president. Both sides claimed that there had been fraud involved in the voting in the unconfirmed states, and many Republicans said that large-scale intimidation of potential black voters by groups like the Red Shirts and the White League meant that the results in these states would not necessarily be fair or representative.

An Electoral Commission was convened, and this voted by a very narrow margin to award all the unconfirmed votes to Hayes, which would make him president. Democrats were outraged and attempted to organize a filibuster to prevent the adoption of the Electoral Commission's findings. With inauguration day approaching, Republican and Democrat politicians met in at Wormley's Hotel in Washington, D.C. to try to negotiate a compromise that would satisfy everyone. Democrats finally agreed that they would accept the findings of the Electoral Commission only if Hayes as president agreed to bring an end to the presence of federal troops in the south and to accept the election of Democratic administrations in the southern states. With this private agreement, Reconstruction was effectively finished.

Even without this agreement, it would have been difficult for the new president to continue Reconstruction. Although Hayes had been a supporter of Reconstruction, the House of Representatives was controlled by a majority of Democrats who simply refused to grant sufficient funds to allow the military control of the southern states to continue. Democrats attempted to have the Enforcement Acts repealed, but Hayes used his veto to prevent this from happening. However, with control of Congress and the Senate, Democrats were able to ensure that no funds were provided to the Federal Marshal Service, the principle way in which laws against groups like the KKK had been enforced. Without funding, it proved very difficult for Hayes to continue with Reconstruction.

Facing continuing intimidation and discrimination as well as a lack of employment opportunities, many African Americans chose to leave the southern states. Some left the United States altogether, going to Liberia and other destinations. Others moved north and west with a large number moving to Kansas from various states along the Mississippi River. These black migrants became known as Exodusters, and by 1890, there were substantial African American populations as far west as Oklahoma, New Mexico, Arizona, Nevada, and California.

For blacks who remained in the south, prospects were poor. Although Reconstruction was never formally ended, the reality was that there were few attempts to enforce the rights of African Americans in the years following the compromise which led to the election of Hayes as president. Black Codes and other racial laws which treated blacks as citizens of lesser importance and with fewer rights remained in place, and racial violence against blacks in the south continued virtually unabated and generally unpunished. Even the KKK made a come-back—by the early years of the twentieth century, the Klan claimed more than four million members. It expanded the range of its bigotry to include hate and violence not just against blacks but also Catholics and Jews.

In the sense of empowering and entitling African Americans, Reconstruction was generally a failure. The situation of most blacks in America in 1877 was little better than it had been in 1865. In some cases it was actually worse. The historian W. E. B. Du Bois wrote, "The slave went free; stood a brief moment in the sun; then moved back again toward slavery." Still, Reconstruction was about more than the abolition of slavery—it was also concerned with reintegrating the formerly rebel southern states into the Union and making them once again part of the United States. In that sense at least, it succeeded.

Conclusion

By the time that the Reconstruction Era ended in 1877, the hopes and dreams of many northerners could be seen to have been optimistic in the extreme and perhaps even naïve. African Americans were no longer slaves, but neither were they equal citizens in many parts of the U.S. Unfair and discriminatory laws were used against them and, in some areas, extreme violence was used to intimidate and suppress black populations.

Yet, though it would be many, many more years before African Americans achieved even legal equality with white Americans, the roots of what became the civil rights movement of the 1960s can be traced back to the Reconstruction Era. Independent black churches, which were such an important part of the civil rights movement, first appeared in the period after the Civil War. Black politicians and black officeholders first appeared in the same period. Black sharecroppers may have struggled to make a living, but they were no longer slaves, and they had won the right to vote.

The Reconstruction Era may not have delivered the utopian society that many had hoped for, but in retrospect it can be seen as an important step toward the eventual granting of civil rights to African Americans.

Made in the USA
San Bernardino, CA
26 November 2019